Language Arts Tutor: Capitalization and Punctuation

By
CINDY BARDEN

COPYRIGHT © 2005 Mark Twain Media, Inc.

ISBN 1-58037-284-8

Printing No. CD-404012

Mark Twain Media, Inc., Publishers
Distributed by Carson-Dellosa Publishing Company, Inc.

Table of Contents

Introduction

Students of all ability levels prefer interesting and readable material, particularly those who struggle with capitalization and punctuation in their writing. The Language Arts Tutor series engages the interests of these students through individualized tutoring in highly readable, age-appropriate activities. The series introduces and strengthens the concepts needed to build and reinforce capitalization and punctuation skills for students in grades four through eight.

The Tutor series comprises an array of titles in reading, math, science, and language arts. Designed in a lively, non-intimidating format, the reproducible activities include stories, exercises, games, riddles, puzzles, and other stimulating materials to improve skills and enrich the learning experience for the struggling learner.

The activities in this book focus on learning capitalization and punctuation guidelines. Capitalization activities include working with names, places, quotations, and titles. Punctuation skills covered include commas, quotation marks, apostrophes, colons, semicolons, dashes, and end punctuation. The proper use of underlining and italics in titles is also discussed.

A sidebar on each page clearly states the capitalization or punctuation concept or skill reinforced by that activity. This format allows students to master one concept or skill at a time, thereby building confidence and proficiency.

Tutors and teachers can meet the special needs of students by selecting specific activities that reinforce the skills each student needs most.

Name: _____ Date: _____

Which Words Are Important?

To **capitalize** means to write the first letter of a word using an uppercase letter.
- Always capitalize the first word of a sentence.
- Capitalize **important words** in names of specific people, places, and things.
- Important words include all nouns, pronouns, verbs, adjectives, and adverbs.
- Unless they are the first word of a sentence or title, do not capitalize: a, an, the, and, or, but, nor, or short prepositions, such as to, of, in, on, and at.
- Capitalize first, last, and middle names of people, including their initials:
  P.T. Barnum
  Mary Ann Evans
- Use periods after a person's initials.
- Capitalize specific names of animals: Lassie
      Shamu
- Capitalize a person's title if it is used immediately before a person's name; otherwise it is lowercase.
  <u>Dr.</u> Marian Lipinowski is a dermatologist.
      An apple a day keeps the <u>doctor</u> away.
- Use a period after a title that is abbreviated.
  Dr.   Mrs.   Capt.

Directions: Rewrite these words and phrases correctly.

1. king arthur

   _____

2. an English Queen

   _____

3. ann brown, president

   _____

4. smokey bear

   _____

5. judge lawson

   _____

6. jumbo, the elephant

   _____

7. sir arthur conan doyle

   _____

8. president and mrs lincoln

   _____

Name: _____ Date: _____

What's in a Name?

Directions: Fill in the blanks with names of people, animals, or characters as indicated.

1. a man
2. a woman
3. a doctor
4. a relative
5. a teacher
6. an author
7. an animal
8. an athlete
9. a friend
10. a cartoon character
11. another animal
12. yourself

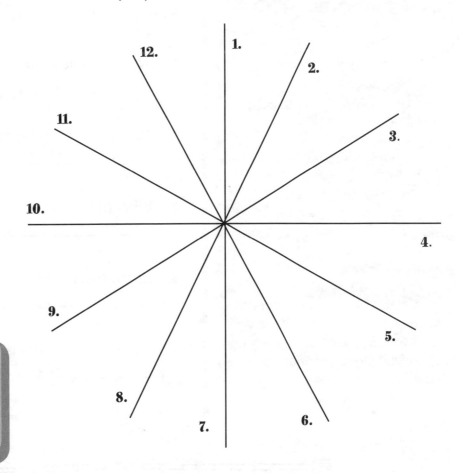

> Many dictionaries indicate words and phrases that should be capitalized. When in doubt, look it up.

Directions: Circle the words that should be capitalized. Add periods where needed.

13. Please join me in welcoming mayor sandra a cummins.

14. Have you met mr peter stone, our next circuit judge?

15. andrew q jorgenson is a professor at the university.

16. prof harlan golfed with dr watson and the governor, thomas j bradley.

17. Why did coach a j brown take the team out for pizza?

18. Have you seen the movie about seabiscuit the racehorse?

19. In the TV show, "star trek: the next generation," mr data had a cat named spot.

Name: _____ Date: _____

Be Wise: Capitalize and Italicize

Capitalize important words in titles of

- books:
  Harry Potter and the Chamber of Secrets
- newspapers:
  Long Island Reporter
- magazines:
  Sports Illustrated
- plays:
  Romeo and Juliet
- movies:
  The Last of the Mohicans

When you type, use italics for titles of books, newspapers, magazines, and plays. Since you can't write in italics, underline when writing longhand.

Directions: Supply the titles requested below. Underline the titles that should be italicized.

1. Write the title of the last book you read.

   _____

2. Name a local newspaper.

   _____

3. What magazine do you enjoy reading?

   _____

4. Name a play.

   _____

5. Write the name of the last movie you saw.

   _____

Name: _____ Date: _____

Capitalize With Quotation Marks

Capitalize important words in the titles of
- songs:
  "The Wheels on the Bus"
- poems:
  "Stopping by Woods on a Snowy Evening"
- stories:
  "Snow White and the Seven Dwarfs"
- TV shows:
  "Gilligan's Island"
- articles in newspapers or magazines:
  "Everything You Always Wanted to Know About Capitalization"
- chapters of books:
  "The Worst Birthday"

Enclose titles of TV shows, songs, poems, stories, articles, and chapters inside quotation marks.

Directions: Rewrite these titles. Use correct capitalization and punctuation. Underline or use quotation marks when needed.

1. song: jingle bells

   _____

2. movie: indiana jones and the temple of doom

   _____

   _____

3. book: cloudy with a chance of meatballs

   _____

4. newspaper: the boston chronicle

   _____

5. magazine: reader's digest

   _____

6. article: 101 things you can do to save our planet

   _____

   _____

7. play: the merchant of venice

   _____

8. story: the emperor's new clothes

   _____

9. poem: ode to the west wind

   _____

10. TV show: ask this old house

    _____

Name: _____   Date: _____

Have You Ever Been to Bologna, Italy?

Capitalize **important words** in the names of

- cities:
  Walla Walla
- counties:
  Milwaukee County
- states and prov-
  inces:
  Hawaii;
  Saskatchewan
- countries:
  Turkey;
  Republic of Haiti
- continents:
  Asia

Separate the names of cities and states with commas.

Barbourville, Kentucky

Separate the names of cities and countries with commas.

Mexico City, Mexico

The city of Lima, Peru, is the nation's capital.

Directions: Use an atlas. Write the names of three cities and their countries or states for each area on the lines next to the map outline. Then place a dot and the corresponding number on the map. Find names that sound interesting or unusual. Lima, Peru, has been done as an example.

SOUTH AMERICA

1. Lima, Peru _____

2. _____

3. _____

ASIA

1. _____

2. _____

3. _____

SCANDINAVIA

1. _____

2. _____

3. _____

AUSTRALIA

1. _____

2. _____

3. _____

Name: _____ Date: _____

Around the World

• Capitalize words derived from the names of cities, states, countries, or continents, such as races, languages, and nationalities.

Bostonians
Texans
Brazilians
French
Africans
Spanish
Greek
English

Directions: Circle the words that should be capitalized.

1. eun-jung translated the korean story into english and ukrainian.
2. Would you like to play chinese checkers or michigan rummy?
3. We ordered a new york-style pizza with spanish olives, italian sausage, french mushrooms, canadian bacon, bermuda onions, mexican peppers, and greek goat cheese.
4. At the swiss embassy party, guests from several canadian provinces met members of the british parliament, several german actors, and a polish singer.
5. Most people in south america speak spanish.
6. brazil was the only latin american country settled by people from portugal, and portuguese is the official language.
7. My aunt rachel collects persian rugs, arabian horses, and mexican pottery.
8. The egyptian pyramids and the hanging gardens of babylon were two of the seven wonders of the ancient world.
9. When elena researched her family tree, she learned that her ancestors included norwegians, swedes, finns, and russians.

10. Many foods we eat include words derived from cities or countries, such as Turkish taffy, French toast, German rye, and Polish sausage. Write the names of other foods that include the names of places.

_____

_____

_____

Name: _____ Date: _____

What's on the Menu?

Directions: Make capitalization corrections to the menu.

SPECIAL OF THE DAY
denver omelet
with swiss cheese and canadian bacon

SOUP OF THE DAY
new England clam chowder
tex-mex chili

SANDWICHES: meatballs on italian bread
polish sausage on german rye
philly cheese steak

SIDE ORDERS: mashed idaho potatoes
with real lumps
french fries
vidalia onion rings
boston baked beans
texas toast
romaine lettuce salad with
russian dressing, bermuda
onions, and roma tomatoes

DESSERTS: boston cream pie
french vanilla ice cream
georgia peach pie

BEVERAGES: columbian coffee
english tea
florida orange juice

Name: _____ Date: _____

Places, Places

Capitalize **important words** in the names of
- planets: Saturn
- stars: Alpha Centari
- galaxies: the Milky Way
- mountain ranges: the Himalayas
- valleys: Pleasant Valley
- canyons: Grand Canyon
- waterfalls: Bridal Falls
- rivers: Mississippi River
- lakes: Buffalo Lake
- volcanoes: Mount Vesuvius
- national parks: Yellowstone National Park

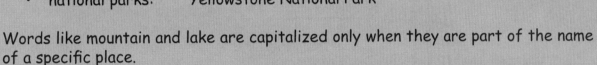

Words like mountain and lake are capitalized only when they are part of the name of a specific place.

We climbed several peaks in the <u>Rocky Mountains</u> and the <u>Appalachian Mountains</u>.
We climbed several <u>mountains</u> in the Alps and Himalayas.

We fished in <u>Lake Michigan</u>, <u>Green Lake</u>, and <u>Lake Winnebago</u>.
We fished in several <u>lakes</u> including Erie, Superior, and Huron.

Directions: Circle the capitalization errors.

1. minnesota has 10,000 Lakes.

2. neptune, uranus, mars, and venus are four of the Planets in our solar system.

3. among the longest Rivers on earth are the amazon, the nile, and the mississippi.

4. did you know that earth is in the milky way galaxy?

5. lake titicaca is located on the border between peru and bolivia.

6. the huge statue of christ on mount corcovado overlooks rio de janeiro.

7. thomas jefferson asked lewis and clark to find a water route to the pacific ocean.

8. meriwether lewis and william clark traveled up the missouri river past the great falls.

                     9

Name: _____   Date: _____

Who Lives at 1600 Pennsylvania Avenue?

- Capitalize **important words** in the names of streets, avenues, boulevards, etc.

   Avenue of the Americas

- Capitalize words such as street, lane, route, and avenue <u>only</u> if they are part of a specific address name.

   She lived on <u>Primrose Lane</u>.
   He strolled down the <u>lane</u>.

- Capitalize the two-letter postal abbreviations for states. Do not use a period.

   Boneyard, AZ

Directions: Should the underlined words be capitalized? Write yes or no on the lines.

1. Hal lived on a busy <u>street</u>. _____

2. Bonnie bought a bungalow on <u>batman boulevard</u>. _____

3. Maureen lives at <u>route</u> 3, Byron, WI. _____

4. The president lives at 1600 <u>pennsylvania avenue</u>. _____

5. Are they building a new <u>highway</u> outside of town? _____

6. My address is 17 <u>crescent circle</u>. _____

7. Send the rebate form to <u>post office box</u> 5493220356475. _____

8. Would you like to live in Toad Suck, <u>ak</u>? _____

9. I can never remember if <u>ak</u> is the abbreviation for Alaska or Arkansas. _____

10. Many of the <u>roads</u> in our county need repair. _____

Name: _____   Date: _____

Which Way?

Directions: Correct the capitalization errors.

1. _____

2. _____

5. _____

6. _____

3. _____

4. _____

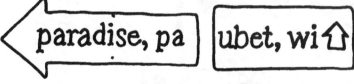

7. _____   8. _____

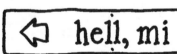

9. _____

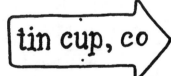

10. _____   11. _____   12. _____

13. _____   14. _____   15. _____

Name: _____ Date: _____

The Short Versions

- **Abbreviations** are shortened forms of words. Use a period at the end of most abbreviations.
  <u>Mr.</u> is an abbreviation for Mister.

- If the word should be capitalized, then capitalize the abbreviation.
  Is Sesame <u>St.</u> a real street?

- Do not use a period at the end of abbreviations for single words if all letters in the abbreviation are capitalized.
  TV   OK

- Most dictionaries list abbreviations for words.

Directions: Write the abbreviations for the underlined words. Use a dictionary or other reference source if you need help.

1. Main <u>Street</u>   _____

2. Second <u>Avenue</u>   _____

3. Pacific <u>Boulevard</u>   _____

4. Worms, <u>Nebraska</u>   _____

5. <u>Father</u> Flanagan   _____

6. <u>Reverend</u> Jackson   _____

7. <u>Mount Saint</u> Helens   _____

8. <u>Doctor</u> Schweitzer   _____

9. <u>Mistress</u> Abernathy   _____

10. <u>Attorney</u> Rachel Cross   _____

11. 47 <u>South</u> 14th Street   _____

12. Winnebago <u>Drive</u>   _____

Name: _____ Date: _____

Mardi Gras Is French for "Fat Tuesday"

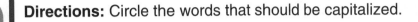

Directions: Circle the words that should be capitalized.

1.	january	new year's day	feast of the three kings
2.	february	valentine's day	groundhog day
3.	march	st. patrick's day	easter sunday
4.	april	all fools' day	passover
5.	may	mother's day	memorial day
6.	june	father's day	flag day
7.	july	independence day	fourth of july
8.	august	sisters' day	lefthander's day
9.	september	labor day	grandparents' day
10.	october	columbus day	halloween
11.	november	thanksgiving day	veterans' day
12.	december	christmas day	hanukkah kwanzaa

Name: _____ Date: _____

Riddle Me

Directions: Circle all words that should be capitalized. Can you answer the riddles?

1. which hand do people in iowa use to eat their soup?

2. why can't a man living in new york be buried west of the mississippi river?

3. if milk is $2.75 a gallon in illinois, what are window panes in missouri?

4. where do math teachers like to visit in new york city?

5. for what should you be thankful on thanksgiving day?

6. before mount everest was discovered, what was the tallest mountain in the world?

7. when does friday come before thursday?

8. on january 1 at 7:15 a.m., fourteen people walked out of the best restaurant in paris, france. Why?

9. in what month do coyotes howl the least?

10. if april showers bring may flowers, then what do may flowers bring?

11. why did santa have only seven reindeer on christmas eve?

12. what do cows in wisconsin do for fun on a saturday night?

13. a man in texas wore red shoes every day for a year. What did they become when he stepped into the rio grande river?

14. a man rode into tombstone, arizona, on his horse. He arrived on friday, spent three days in town, and left on friday. How is this possible?

15. what do people in devonshire, england, call baby cats?

16. which candles burn longer: white ones in spain or blue ones in germany?

17. why did cowboys in new mexico ride their horses to town?

Name: _____ Date: _____

Do You Prefer NBA or MLB Games?

• **Acronyms** are words made from the first letters of a group of words. Usually the word is pronounced by saying the name of each letter.

• Capitalize all letters in acronyms. Do not use periods.

Directions: Use a dictionary or other reference source to complete the acronym chart.

	Acronym	Meaning
1.	ASAP	as soon as possible
2.	_____	Central Intelligence Agency
3.	_____	cash on delivery
4.	GI	_____
5.	IRS	_____
6.	NBC	_____
7.	_____	National Football League
8.	PM	_____
9.	PS	_____
10.	_____	registered nurse
11.	RV	_____
12.	_____	self-contained underwater breathing apparatus
13.	_____	unidentified flying object
14.	_____	very important person

Sometimes small words are omitted in acronyms.

15.	BLT	bacon, lettuce, and tomato
16.	FBI	_____
17.	NASA	_____

Name: _____ Date: _____

A Little More of This and That

Directions: Fill in the blanks with another example of each type.

Capitalize important words in the names of:

- political parties: Democrats   _____

- religious groups: Latter-Day Saints   _____

- formal groups: Knights of Columbus   _____

- organizations: Girl Scouts   _____

- schools: Adams Middle School   _____

- universities   University of Maine   _____

- colleges   Boston College   _____

- monuments: Lincoln Memorial   _____

- famous buildings: Empire State Building   _____

- ships: U.S.S. *Arizona*   _____

- computer programs/software: Outlook Express   _____

- government departments: Department of Justice   _____

- famous documents: Bill of Rights   _____

- major historical periods   the Middle Ages   _____

- major events in history: the Great Depression   _____

- wars: Revolutionary War   _____

- battles: Battle of Gettysburg   _____

Name: _____ Date: _____

Odds and Ends

- Capitalize the first word in the **salutation** of a letter:
  <u>Dear</u> Mary,

- Capitalize the first word in the **closing** of a letter:
  <u>Yours</u> truly,

- Capitalize the important words in brand names and use the trademark symbol:
  Colgate™

- Capitalize important words in the nicknames of people, animals, places, or things:
  King of Swat
  Rex, the Wonder Dog
  City of Angels
  Old Faithful

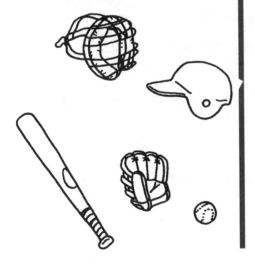

Directions: Underline the words that should be capitalized.

dear sid,

did you see the baseball history special on tv last night? my favorite story was the one about "shoeless" joe jackson. he began his baseball career as a pitcher, but became an outfielder because his fastball was so forceful it once broke a catcher's arm, and nobody would agree to catch for him.

you knew I was named for stan "the man" musial, the famous rightfielder and first baseman for the st. louis cardinals, didn't you? my middle name, louis, came from the "iron horse," lou gehrig.

my dad played minor league ball for a while and has always been a great baseball fan. he couldn't decide whether to name me ty, after the "georgia peach," ty cobb, or joe, after "joltin'" joe dimaggio. mom refused to consider the name george for george herman ruth because she thought a nickname like "babe" wouldn't be all that great when I grew up.

maybe this summer we can head up to the windy city and watch the cubbies play at wrigley field.

your cousin,

stan

Name: _____ Date: _____

Proofread the Trivia

Directions: Circle the words that need to be capitalized in the following sentences. The number of errors is included in brackets ([ ]) at the end of each sentence.

1. people who live in naples, italy, are called neopolitans. [4]

2. some cities with unusual names include embarrass, mn; square butt, mt; and echo, tx. [8]

3. did you know that the full name of the wonderful cartoon duck created by walt disney was donald fauntleroy duck? [6]

4. some of the villains in the tv show, "batman," included king tut, the joker, the archer, the black widow, the mad hatter, and the clock king. [13]

5. adam west played the part of batman, and burt ward played his sidekick, robin, the boy wonder. [8]

6. andy griffith, better known as sheriff andy taylor, never won an emmy for either of his popular tv shows: "the andy griffith show" or "matlock." [12]

7. don knotts, who played deputy barney fife, won five emmys for his supporting role. [6]

8. before lassie became the heroine of a popular tv show, she was the main character in a short novel titled, *lassie come home*, written by eric mowbray knight. [9]

9. caryn johnson made her first appearance on stage at the helena rubenstein children's theatre in new york city at the age of 8. [9]

10. you may not recognize the name caryn johnson, but you might know her by her stage name, whoopi goldberg. [5]

Name: _____ Date: _____

Capitalize It! Word Search

Directions: Find and circle the types of words that should be capitalized. The words in the puzzle may be printed up, down, forward, backward, or diagonally.

battles	books	cities	colleges	days	documents
lakes	months	monuments	mountains	movies	names
oceans	parks	planets	poems	rivers	schools
seas	ships	songs	states	stories	valleys
wars					

```
Y X U H P S V Y Y O E G N P M N N J D B L M B C
G H Q F U O W K Z K I X B E J M L A G M E G P P
H N D R Y C E Z O G X V Y Y O S K O O B W U J F
S T A T E S N M R F I M S U Q U Z Z C C J O I M
H B Z R S Y Z I S T F F N Y R I V E R S A C C W
V P Z I B A T T L E S T M G I Y K O T Z Q N O G
W V B W U C L L L P A I M W S G L E E T L G L U
A F T R E E M O V I E S R D Q T O Q J E A C L C
B N A M E S S C N U B R S H Y D N K F U K Z E S
W Z A I Q T H S R X E N B B C X E E X X E O G S
O G A V O X T N T K A Q U I L F J G M U S C E W
Y R G R M A Z A N E O A H I B C Y O D U Q S S F
K X I I E J A M C E I A L C V K E P A G C L G R
N E Y U S J I O D A B L Y Y D O J P L H A O E Y
S R G S U Z A L G A H S E B K Z P I B A A W D O
S S J R S H C Q B O Y C K C S Q E C T S N E G T
Y G R A Y M A K J N Z S N R N P B T A O Z E M Q
E S O W C O V Y A O F S E N A H I G R N E C T P
L B K M Z N L M X W A H L A X P S H G G U N A S
L E P K V T L P M I W K U O S H K E S S R J F K
A F R H W H Z F C E W L Y Z O D R I I T Z C O C
V K D D I S G C Q A L H T V E H M A R T R N Y F
X E A P Z T D T K F G Y N Z X S C D P C I J M J
S T N E M U N O M J K B N T P E J S Y U M C A K
```

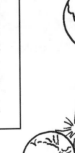

List three other types of words that should be capitalized.

_____

_____

Name: _____ Date: _____

At the End

All sentences end with punctuation.

- Sentences that state a fact or a command end with a **period**.

    Gorillas rarely wash their hands after eating.
    Wash the gorilla's hands before you leave, Glen.

- Sentences that ask a question end with a **question mark**.

    Glen, did you remember to wash the gorilla's hands?

- Sentences that show strong emotion or surprise end with an **exclamation point**.

    Wow! That gorilla has really clean hands!

Directions: Add punctuation to the end of each sentence. Circle all the words where there is a capitalization error.

1. Who gave the zebra a bath

2. Oh, oh! Look what happened

3. Paint the stripes on the zebras before you go to lunch

4. Did you know that a hippopotamus can run faster than a person

5. The word *hippopotamus* means "water horse" in greek

6. Hummingbirds can fly backwards

7. fill the hummingbird feeder with sugar water

8. Look, There are six hummingbirds at the feeder already

9. Do you know which land animal is the tallest

10. At birth, a baby giraffe is six feet tall

11. That's a very tall baby

12. giraffes were called "camel leopards" by the Romans

Name: _____ Date: _____

Commas Separate

- Use a **comma** to separate the number of the day of the month and the year.

  Abraham Lincoln was born on February 12, 1809.
  December 7, 1941, was the date of the attack on Pearl Harbor.

- Do not use a comma to separate the month and year if no date is given.

  George Washington was born in February 1732.

- Use **commas** to separate three or more words in a series.

  Mia ordered spaghetti, garlic bread, a salad, and a soda.

- Use a **comma** to separate cities from states, provinces, and/or other countries.

  Monkey's Eyebrow, Kentucky
  Attawapiskat, Ontario, Canada
  Rome, Italy
  Jefferson City, Missouri, is the capital of the state.

Directions: Add commas to the following sentences.

1. Thomas Jefferson, born on April 13 1743, in Shadwell Virginia, became the third president in March 1801.

2. Jefferson died on July 4 1826, and was buried at his home near Charlottesville Virginia.

3. Born in Hyde Park New Jersey in January 1882, Franklin D. Roosevelt died on April 12 1945, shortly after he began his fourth term as president.

4. Three different men served as vice president with Franklin Roosevelt: John N. Garner Henry A. Wallace and Harry S Truman.

5. While president, Richard M. Nixon traveled to Moscow Russia, and Beijing China.

6. Theodore Roosevelt had six children: Alice Theodore Kermit Ethel Archibald and Quentin.

Name: _____ Date: _____

Dendrophobia, A Fear of Trees

• Use **commas** to separate nouns or pronouns in **direct address** from the rest of the sentence. A noun or pronoun in direct address is one that names or refers to the person addressed.

Glen, your gorilla is a disgrace!
Your gorilla, Glen, is a disgrace!
Your gorilla is a disgrace, Glen!

• Use **commas** to seprate appositives from the rest of the sentence. **Appositives** are words that provide more information about a previous noun or pronoun.

Glen, the boy with the pet gorilla, is my neighbor.

Directions: Underline the noun or pronoun used in direct address. Add commas.

1. Barry you have to get over your barophobia if you ever hope to become an astronaut.

2. Listen, Barry barophobia means fear of gravity.

3. Do you have any other phobias Barry?

4. "Santa Claus I'd like you to meet my friend, Jeanine," said the littlest elf.

5. "Jeanine might be shy Santa because she has pogonophobia, a fear of beards," he explained.

Directions: Underline the word or words used as appositives. Add commas.

6. Boston the city sometimes called Bean Town is the capital of Massachusetts.

7. Calvin Coolidge known as Silent Cal installed a mechanical horse in the White House and liked to bounce around on it, whooping like a cowboy at a rodeo.

8. Harriet Tubman nicknamed the "Moses of her people" led many slaves to freedom on the Underground Railroad.

9. Besides being a writer and a politician, Benjamin Franklin the man who invented bifocals also invented lightning rods.

10. Acrophobia the fear of heights is rather common, but alektorophobia the fear of chickens is quite rare.

Name: _____ Date: _____

Two Into One

- Use a **comma** to separate independent clauses in a compound sentence joined by the words and, for, or, nor, or but.

- An **independent clause** is a group of words that makes a complete thought. Each independent clause could be a complete sentence by itself.

  <u>Doug ate a cheese pizza for lunch</u>, and <u>he ordered a cup of raspberry cappuccino to go</u>, but <u>he decided to play hooky</u>, and <u>he did not return to his office</u>.

- If the independent clauses are very short (two or three words), a comma is not needed.

  <u>He told jokes</u> but <u>she didn't laugh</u>.

Directions: Join the independent clauses to make one sentence joined by *and, for, or, nor,* or *but.* Rewrite the sentences using commas where needed.

1. Abby raked the leaves into piles. Andy put the leaves into bags.

   _____

   _____

   _____

2. Beth wanted to spend the day at the mall. She also wanted to spend the day at the beach.

   _____

   _____

   _____

3. Carlos fixed my bicycle. He could not fix my car.

   _____

   _____

4. Diane ate three helpings of spaghetti for supper. She was too full for dessert.

   _____

   _____

   _____

5. Ethan ran a good race. Ellen finished in first place.

   _____

   _____

6. Chuck washed the windows of his '57 Chevy. He checked the oil. He forgot to fill it with gas.

   _____

   _____

   _____

Name: _____ Date: _____

A Few More Ways to Use Commas

- Use a comma after the **salutation** in a friendly letter.
  Dear John,

- Use a comma after the **closing** in a letter.
  Your friend,

- Use a comma after **introductory phrases**.
  After Consuela finished sweeping, the wind began to blow.

- The meaning of a sentence can completely change if commas are missing. Use a comma to show that Consuela did not sweep the wind. Without a comma in the following sentence, it would seem that Marco ate the sea gulls.
  As Marco ate, the sea gulls circled, waiting for crumbs.

- Use a comma after **yes or no** when it is the first word in a sentence.
  Yes, Abraham Lincoln was born in a log cabin.
  No, George Washington didn't chop down a cherry tree.

Directions: Add commas where needed.

1. When we cooked the people in the apartment next to us complained about the smell.

2. When we barbecued the neighbor's dog barked.

3. While the children ate the horses grazed.

4. If grandma bakes the children will have homemade gingerbread for dessert.

5. No we aren't in Kansas anymore.

6. Before you vacuum the goldfish bowl should be cleaned.

7. Dear Santa

8. Yours truly

9. Since Dave left the house seems much quieter.

10. Because Kathy stopped the turtle was not crushed by the car.

Name: _____ Date: _____

What Did They Say?

• A **quotation** contains the exact words written or spoken by someone. Quotation marks show when the person's words begin and end.

   Comedian Groucho Marx once said, "Outside of a dog, a book is man's best friend. Inside of a dog, it's too dark to read."

• Use a **comma** to set off words such as he said and she replied that are not part of the quotation.

   Snoopy said, "Yesterday, I was a dog. Today, I'm a dog. Tomorrow, I'll probably still be a dog. Sigh! There's so little hope for advancement."

• If a quotation is a **complete sentence**, put end-of-sentence punctuation inside the quotation marks.

   Douglas Adams, author of Hitchhiker's Guide to the Galaxy wrote, "The ships hung in the sky in much the same way that bricks don't."

• If a quotation is **not complete**, put a comma inside the quotation marks, followed by the rest of the quotation.

   "Show me a sane man," said Carl Jung, "and I will cure him for you."

Directions: Use the examples at the right as guidelines. Add quotation marks, commas, and end-of-sentence punctuation as needed.

1. After serving one term as president, Calvin Coolidge stated I do not choose to run for President in 1928

2. When asked why, Coolidge replied Because there's no chance for advancement

3. There, I guess King George will be able to read that stated John Hancock after he signed his name in large letters on the Declaration of Independence.

4. People who are wrapped up in themselves make small packages wrote Benjamin Franklin.

5. Now that I realize what they've had to put up with wrote Betty Ford about being the first lady I have a new respect and admiration for every one of them

Name: _____ Date: _____

Yogi-isms

I didn't really say everything I said.

Directions: Add punctuation to these quotes by former baseball star, Yogi Berra.

1. A nickel ain't worth a dime anymore he complained

2. It's never happened in World Series history, and it hasn't happened since Yogi told fans

3. It's déjà vu all over again he exclaimed

4. Yogi advised When you come to a fork in the road, take it

5. He also said We're lost but we're making good time

6. If I didn't wake up I'd still be sleeping he said

7. Some of Yogi's advice was confusing, like the time he said Always go to other people's funerals; otherwise, they won't go to yours

8. Little League baseball is a good thing 'cause it keeps the parents off the streets and it keeps the kids out of the house! he told a reporter

9. The future ain't what it used to be Yogi said, and I think he was right

Name: _____ Date: _____

A Dark and Stormy Night

Directions: First, circle the letter of the sentence in each group that is completely correct. Then, briefly describe the punctuation error found in each of the other sentences in the group.

Group 1

A. Jake, woke suddenly in the middle of a dark and stormy night.

_____

B. Thunder boomed and lightning flashed!

_____

C. What were those sounds coming from his closet.

_____

D. Jake reached for his glasses but he could not find them.

_____

Group 2

A. Meanwhile, the small furry creature trapped in the closet tried to get Jake's attention.

_____

B. Let me out, it called in small furry creature talk.

_____

C. Lightning flared casting strange shadows on the walls and ceiling.

_____

D. Thunder shook the house?

_____

Group 3

A. After the thunder the silence seemed ominous.

_____

B. When Jake finally found his glasses and switched on the lamp beside his bed he found himself in a strange room.

_____

C. His bed his dresser his posters and even his stinky dirty clothes were gone.

_____

D. "Let me out of here!" boomed a loud voice from behind a door near the bed.

_____

Name: _____ Date: _____

Shouldn't, Wouldn't, Couldn't

- A contraction contains two words joined to-gether to make a shorter word.

- Use an apostrophe to show one or more missing letters.

- Many contractions contain a pronoun and a verb.

- Some contractions in-clude a verb and the word not.

Directions: Complete the pronoun/verb contractions below.

	Pronoun		Verb		Contraction
1.	I	+	am	=	I'm
2.	we	+	are	=	we're
	you	+	are	=	you're
	they	+	are	=	_____
3.	he	+	is	=	he's
	she	+	is	=	_____
	it	+	is	=	it's
4.	I	+	have	=	I've
	we	+	have	=	_____
	you	+	have	=	you've
	they	+	have	=	_____

5.	I	+	would	I'd		6.	I	+	will	_____
	you	+	would	_____			you	+	will	_____
	we	+	would	we'd			we	+	will	_____
	she	+	would	_____			she	+	will	_____
	he	+	would	he'd			he	+	will	_____
	they	+	would	_____			they	+	will	_____

Directions: Finish the verb/not contractions below.

7. did + not = _____
8. should + not = _____
9. had + not = _____
10. will + not = _____
11. _____ + _____ = wouldn't
12. _____ + _____ = couldn't
13. _____ + _____ = haven't
14. _____ + _____ = shan't

SHAN'T shouldn't couldn't wouldn't

28

Name: _____ Date: _____

Contraction Action

Directions: Circle the correct answers.

1. will not
   A. wil'nt   B. wiln't   C. wo'nt   D. won't

2. we would
   A. we'ed   B. we'ld   C. we'd   D. we'l'd

3. shouldn't
   A. shall not   B. should have   C. should not   D. shall have

4. they're
   A. their   B. they are   C. there are   D. their are

5. you are
   A. your   B. your'e   C. yo're   D. you're

6. we are
   A. were   B. we're   C. wer're   D. we'are

7. I am
   A. I'm   B. I'am   C. I'll   D. I'd

8. don't
   A. dough not   B. do not   C. did not   D. done not

9. can't
   A. cannot   B. could not   C. she can   D. they cannot

10. she will
   A. shel'l   B. shell   C. she'll   D. she'ill

Name: _____ Date: _____

What's Your Favorite Phobia?

Directions: Write the contractions for the underlined words.

1. Rocky and Moose <u>are not</u> going to the apiary because they have apiphobia, a fear of bees.

    _____

2. <u>I have</u> never heard of anyone having arachibutyrophobia, a fear of peanut butter sticking

    to the roof of one's mouth. _____

3. <u>He is</u> never going to become an astronaut because he has siderophobia, a fear of the

    stars, and cometophobia, a fear of comets. _____

4. Abby <u>will not</u> march in the parade because she has aulophobia, a fear of flutes.

    _____

5. Who <u>would have</u> thought that a librarian could develop bibliophobia, a fear of books?

    _____

6. By the time Anne finishes cleaning her room, <u>she will</u> have blennophobia, a fear of slime.

    _____

7. I know Samantha <u>does not</u> have catoptrophobia, a fear of mirrors.

    _____

8. <u>Do not</u> move to Alaska if you have chionophobia, a fear of snow, or cryophobia, a fear of

    ice or frost. _____

9. <u>You had</u> better not move to an island if you have gephyrophobia, a fear of crossing bridges.

    _____

10. The twins always stay together because <u>they are</u> afraid of empty rooms. (kenophobia)

    _____

11. People who want to become mechanics <u>should not</u> have mechanophobia, a fear of ma-

    chinery. _____

12. <u>What is</u> his problem? <u>It is</u> called tonitrophobia and means a fear of thunder.

    _____   _____

Name: _____ Date: _____

Fine as Frog's Fur

- Use an **apostrophe** to show possession when writing about something that belongs to someone or something.

- If the noun is singular, add an apostrophe and an s at the end of the word.
  <u>frog's</u> fur
  <u>Ross's</u> rhinoceros

- The word that names what is owned can be singular or plural.

  A singular noun with one item:
  the <u>lady's</u> lizard
  (One lady has one lizard.)

  A singular noun with more than one item:
  the <u>lady's</u> leopards
  (One lady has more than one leopard.)

- If using the possessive form of a noun sounds weird or wrong, as in number 9 at the right, you can reword your sentence using a possessive pronoun.

  Correct, but awkward: The <u>mouse's houses</u> were inside the wall.

  Rewritten using a possessive pronoun: The mouse had <u>its houses</u> inside the wall.

Directions: Rewrite the phrases using the possessive form of the noun. The first one is done as an example.

1. one man has more than one monkey:
   man's monkeys
   _____

2. Oscar has one orange octopus:
   _____

3. Dr. Seuss has more than one story:
   _____

4. a child has several grandparents:
   _____

5. Agnes has more than one ache:
   _____

6. a fly has more than one wing:
   _____

7. a zebra has more than one stripe:
   _____

8. Pat has one pair of pajamas:
   _____

9. a mouse has more than one house:
   _____

10. a goose has more than one egg:
   _____

Name: _____ Date: _____

Are There Mice in Their Houses?

- Use an **apostrophe** to show possession when writing about something that belongs to someone or something.

- If the noun is plural and ends in an s, add an apostrophe at the end of the word.
    the <u>boys'</u> team

- If the noun is plural and does not end in an s, add an apostrophe and an s.
    the <u>people's</u> choice

- The word that names what is owned can be singular or plural.
    Plural noun with one item that belongs to all of them:
    the <u>children's</u> mother
    (more than one child with the same mother)

    Plural noun with more than one item:
    the <u>ladies'</u> gardens
    (more than one lady and more than one garden)

- If using the possessive form of a noun sounds weird or wrong, as in number 8 to the right, you can reword your sentence.

    Correct, but awkward: The mice's houses were inside the wall.

    Rewritten using a possessive pronoun: The mice had their houses inside the wall.

Directions: Rewrite the phrases using the possessive form of the noun.

1. more than one goose has more than one egg:

    _____

2. one woman belonging to several clubs:

    _____

3. more than one woman belonging to one club:

    _____

4. more than one bird with more than one nest:

    _____

5. grandparents with more than one grandchild:

    _____

6. one fly with more than one eye:

    _____

7. more than one fly has more than one eye:

    _____

8. more than one mouse having more than one house:

    _____

Name: _____ Date: _____

They Lost Their Snake

- **Possessive pronouns** take the place of possessive nouns.
  Amy lost <u>Amy's</u> dog.
  Amy lost <u>her</u> dog.

- Do not use an apostrophe to show possession with pronouns. Instead, use the possessive form of the pronoun.

  Possessive pronouns are:

  Singular
  my, mine
  your, yours
  his, her, hers, its

  Plural
  our, ours
  your, yours
  their, theirs

Directions: Write possessive pronouns to complete the sentences correctly.

1. That apple is Ashley's. It is _____.

2. Ashley took a bite of _____ apple.

3. I bought a CD player. It is _____.

4. I brought _____ CD player to the party.

5. You won the contest, so the prize is _____.

6. When you leave, don't forget to take _____ prize.

7. The dog chased _____ tail, but it did not catch it.

8. Eduardo left _____ new baseball mitt outside in the rain.

9. On the way to the party, they lost _____ pet snake.

10. If you find a lost snake, you will know it is _____.

LOST SNAKE

20-foot boa constrictor named Clyde. Likes to hide under beds. Caution: if found, do not hug. Clyde will hug back. Please call 555-5555.

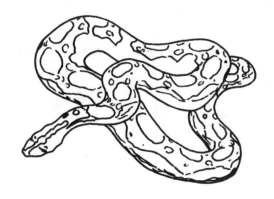

Name: _____ Date: _____

It's Time to Call the Vet

- Don't confuse contractions with possessive pronouns.

Contractions
It's means it is.
You're means you are.
They're means they are.
There's means there is.

Possessive Pronouns
Its means something belongs to it.
Your means something belongs to you.
Their means something belongs to them.
Theirs means it belongs to them.

Directions: Circle the correct words.

1. (It's, Its) time for the dog to take (it's, its) medicine.

2. (Your, You're) going to get (your, you're) reward soon.

3. (Their, They're) lending us (their, they're) DVD player.

4. The problem is (theirs, there's), and (theirs, there's) no one who can help.

Directions: Write possessive pronouns or contractions in the blanks to finish the sentences.

5. _____ too bad that your dog is sick.
6. Have you taken _____ dog to the vet?
7. _____ a new vet on Main Street.
8. Is your dog too sick to wag _____ tail?
9. I'm sure _____ worried about it.
10. Most dog owners become concerned when _____ pets are ill.
11. Max and Frieda were very upset when _____ had to stay at the animal hospital overnight.
12. Aren't you glad the vet said _____ nothing seriously wrong with your dog?

Name: _____ Date: _____

Gus's Goose

Directions: Write the singular possessive form of the noun. Then add a singular noun to show possession. *Example:* Gus   Gus's goose

1. child   _____   _____
2. woman   _____   _____
3. Rosie   _____   _____
4. group   _____   _____
5. squirrel   _____   _____

Directions: Write the plural possessive form of the noun. Then add a singular noun to show possession. *Example:* animal   animals' home

6. crowd   _____   _____
7. man   _____   _____
8. leaf   _____   _____
9. glass   _____   _____
10. aardvark   _____   _____

Directions: Write the singular possessive form of the noun. Then add a plural noun to show possession. *Example:* Gus   Gus's geese

11. person   _____   _____
12. singer   _____   _____
13. frog   _____   _____
14. kitty   _____   _____
15. Cathy   _____   _____

Directions: Write the plural possessive form of the noun. Then add a plural noun to show possession. *Example:* animal   animals' homes

16. fox   _____   _____
17. monkey   _____   _____
18. kitty   _____   _____
19. daisy   _____   _____
20. wolf   _____   _____

Name: _____ Date: _____

Introducing: The Colon

- The main purpose of a colon is to introduce something.

- A colon can introduce a word, a phrase, a sentence, or a list.

Jamal had only one thing on his mind: <u>winning</u>. (a word)

Jamal had only one thing on his mind: <u>winning the game</u>. (a phrase)

Jamal had only one thing on his mind: <u>he wanted to win the game</u>. (a sentence)

Jamal had three things on his mind: <u>finding a receiver, passing the ball, and scoring points</u>. (a list)

Directions: Insert colons where needed. Not all sentences will need colons.

1. For years Jan had saved her money for a reason to take a trip to Hawaii.

2. Jan knew exactly what she wanted to do in Hawaii visit a volcano, swim in the ocean, and visit a pineapple plantation.

3. When Jan visited the island of Oahu, she couldn't believe what she saw a gigantic windmill with blades 400 feet long!

4. Jan tried a new food that she really enjoyed *poi*, a type of dip popular in Hawaii and the South Pacific.

5. To make *poi*, these ingredients are cooked together sweet potatoes and bananas or taro root.

6. After cooking the ingredients until they are soft, *poi* is mashed with water.

7. Traditionally, after preparing *poi*, Hawaiians allow it to sit for a few days until it ferments and turns sour.

8. Jan learned this fact about our fiftieth state more than one-third of the world's pineapple is grown in Hawaii.

9. Coffee is grown in only one of the fifty states Hawaii.

10. Three states do not change over to daylight saving time Arizona, Indiana, and Hawaii.

Name: _____ Date: _____

Five More Ways to Use a Colon

- Use a colon after the **salutation** of a business letter.

    Dear Sir:

- Use a colon between the hour and the minute when writing time.

    School ends at 3:30.

- Use a colon between chapters and verses of the Bible.

    "Friends always show their love. What are brothers for if not to share troubles?" (Proverbs 17:17)

- Use a colon to separate the act from the scene of a play.
    My favorite scene from a Shakespearean play is the one with the three witches in Macbeth I:1.

- Use a colon to separate the title from the subtitle of a book.

    Have you ever read The Story of Harriet Tubman: Conductor of the Underground Railroad?

Directions: Circle the incorrect punctuation and insert a colon instead.

1. Meet me at 3–45, and we'll head for the mall.

2. "An honest answer is the sign of true friendship."

    (Proverbs 24,26)

3. I enjoyed reading *Seabiscuit. An American Legend*.

4. Dear Mr. President,

5. "Be not afraid of greatness. Some are born great,

    some achieve greatness, and some have greatness

    thrust upon 'em." (*Twelfth Night* II,5)

Directions: Use the Internet or other reference sources to find a quotation from a play or the Bible. Write the quotation and its source. Use quotation marks and a colon.

6. _____

    _____

    _____

    _____

    _____

    _____

    _____

Name: _____ Date: _____

Connector and Super Comma

- A **semicolon** signals a reader to pause longer than for a comma, but not as long as for a period. You could call it a "super comma."

- Use a **semicolon** to connect closely related independent clauses not joined by and, or, nor, for, yet, or but. Often the second clause makes a comment on the first clause.

An **independent clause** is a group of words that makes a complete thought. Each independent clause could be a complete sentence by itself.

She lost her marbles; he found them.
The film was excellent; it won many awards.

Remember, when two independent clauses are joined by a conjunction (and, or, nor, for, yet, or but), use a comma.

Directions: Insert a comma or semicolon to separate the independent clauses in each sentence.

1. Little Bo Peep had three sheep but she lost them.

2. She left them alone they came back home.

3. Mary had a little lamb it followed her to school.

4. The mouse ran up the clock and the clock struck one.

5. The little dog laughed the dish ran away with the spoon.

6. The sheep are in the meadow and the cows are in the corn.

7. Jack be nimble Jack be quick.

8. Jack and Jill went up the hill and then they tumbled down.

9. In her garden, she grew silver bells and cockleshells but she didn't grow any oats, peas, beans, or barley.

10. There once was a woman who lived in a shoe yet she and her children lived happily ever after.

Name: _____ Date: _____

Don't Wait to Punctuate

- A semicolon is a super comma between items in a list that already contains commas.

  The rock group played in Little Rock, Arkansas; Rockford, Illinois; Lone Rock, Texas; Slippery Rock, Pennsylvania; and Rock Springs, Wyoming.

- Use a dash (—) to separate words in the middle of a sentence to indicate a sudden change of thought.

  I want a hot dog—no, make that a hamburger—for lunch.

- Use a dash (—) to attach material to the end of a sentence when there is a clean break in continuity.

  Wear your old clothes—new ones might get spoiled.

  Caution: Use dashes sparingly.

Directions: Review the uses of colons, semicolons, and dashes, and then insert them correctly in the following.

1. I'll pick you up at 730 no make it 710 and we'll go rock climbing.

2. The pilot flew to Rome, Italy Frankfurt, Germany Paris, France and London, England last week.

3. Let's follow the west trail or would you rather not?

4. All the people from the village men, women, children joined the animals fleeing the out-of-control fire.

5. Lincoln was a tall man who wore a top hat a most unusual sight to be sure.

6. I'd like a chocolate shake better make that a diet soda I'm trying to lose weight.

7. Dear Library Director

8. Would you please order more historical fiction like *The Black Flower A Novel of the Civil War* for our library?

Name: _____ Date: _____

How Does Your Garden Grow?

Directions: Write a short sentence about plants, trees, or flowers using the type of punctuation shown.

Quotation marks _____

_____

Question mark _____

_____

Apostrophe _____

_____

Colon _____

_____

Comma _____

_____

Exclamation point _____

_____

Semicolon _____

_____

Dash _____

_____

Name: _____ Date: _____

Let's Review

Directions: Write the letter of the correct word(s) in each blank.

1. Capitalize the _____ of specific people, places, and things.

2. Use a(n) _____ at the end of a sentence that asks a question.

3. Use a(n) _____ at the end of a sentence that states a fact.

4. SCUBA is an example of a(n) _____.

5. _____ are shortened forms of two words joined together to make one word.

6. _____ are shortened forms of words.

7. Use a(n) _____ to introduce a word, phrase, sentence, or list.

8. Usually add a(n) _____ and an *s* to show possession.

9. Use a(n) _____ to separate the names of cities and states.

10. A(n) _____ is the exact words someone said.

11. A(n) _____ shows strong emotion.

12. Titles of books are written in _____.

13. Capitalize _____ words in book titles.

14. _____ are contractions.

15. _____ are possessive pronouns.

16. Use a(n) _____ to show a sudden change of thought.

A. Abbreviations

B. Acronym

C. Apostrophe

D. Colon

E. Comma

F. Contractions

G. Dash

H. Exclamation point

I. Important

J. Italics

K. Names

L. Period

M. Question Mark

N. Quotation

O. Theirs and its

P. They're and you're

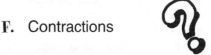
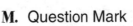

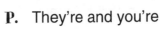

Answer Keys

Which Words Are Important? (p. 2)
1. King Arthur
2. an English queen
3. Ann Brown, president
4. Smokey Bear
5. Judge Lawson
6. Jumbo, the elephant
7. Sir Arthur Conan Doyle
8. President and Mrs. Lincoln

What's in a Name? (p. 3)
1–12. Answers will vary.
13. Mayor Sandra A. Cummins
14. Mr. Peter Stone
15. Andrew Q. Jorgensen
16. Prof. Harlan; Dr. Watson; Thomas J. Bradley
17. Coach A. J. Brown
18. Seabiscuit
19. "Star Trek: The Next Generation,"; Mr. Data; Spot

Be Wise: Capitalize and Italicize (p. 4)
Answers will vary.

Capitalize With Quotation Marks (p. 5)
1. "Jingle Bells"
2. *Indiana Jones and the Temple of Doom*
3. *Cloudy With a Chance of Meatballs*
4. *The Boston Chronicle*
5. *Reader's Digest*
6. "101 Things You Can Do to Save Our Planet"
7. *The Merchant of Venice*
8. "The Emperor's New Clothes"
9. "Ode to the West Wind"
10. "Ask This Old House"

Have You Ever Been to Bologna, Italy? (p. 6)
Answers will vary.

Around the World (p. 7)
1. Eun-Jung; Korean; English; Ukrainian
2. Chinese Checkers; Michigan Rummy
3. New York; Spanish; Italian; French; Canadian; Bermuda; Mexican; Greek
4. Swiss; Canadian; British Parliament; German; Polish
5. South America; Spanish
6. Brazil; Latin American; Portugal; Portuguese
7. Aunt Rachel; Persian; Arabian; Mexican
8. Egyptian; Hanging Gardens; Babylon
9. Elena; Norwegians; Swedes; Finns; Russians
10. Answers will vary.

What's on the Menu? (p. 8)
Denver omelet with Swiss cheese and Canadian bacon
New England clam chowder
Tex-Mex chili
meatballs on Italian bread
Polish sausage on German rye
Philly cheese steak
mashed Idaho potatoes with real lumps
French fries
Vidalia onion rings
Boston baked beans
Texas toast
Romaine lettuce salad with Russian dressing, Bermuda onions, and Roma tomatoes
Boston cream pie
French vanilla ice cream
Georgia peach pie
Colombian coffee
English tea
Florida orange juice

Places, Places (p. 9)
1. Minnesota; lakes
2. Neptune; Uranus; Mars; Venus; planets
3. Among; rivers; Earth; Amazon; Nile; Mississippi
4. Did; Earth; Milky Way
5. Lake Titicaca; Peru; Bolivia
6. The; Christ; Mount Corcovado; Rio; Janeiro
7. Thomas Jefferson; Lewis; Clark; Pacific Ocean
8. Meriwether Lewis; William Clark; Missouri River; Great Falls

Who Lives at 1600 Pennsylvania Avenue? (p. 10)
1. no 2. yes 3. yes
4. yes 5. no 6. yes
7. yes 8. yes 9. yes
10. no

Which Way? (p. 11)
1. Delicious Drive
2. Almond Avenue
3. Highway of Honey
4. Fudge Freeway
5. Spearmint Street
6. Banana Boulevard
7. Cocoa Circle
8. Candy Court
9. Chocolate Avenue
10. Hell, MI
11. Paradise, PA
12. Ubet, WI
13. Tin Cup, CO
14. Gas, KS
15. Cowyard, MS

The Short Versions (p. 12)

1.	St.	2.	Ave.	3.	Blvd.
4.	NE	5.	Fr.	6.	Rev.
7.	Mt. St.	8.	Dr.	9.	Mrs.
10.	Atty.	11.	S.	12.	Dr.

Mardi Gras Is French for "Fat Tuesday" (p. 13)

All words listed should be capitalized except the words *of* and *the* in the holiday *Feast of the Three Kings* and the word *of* in *Fourth of July*.

Riddle Me (p. 14)

Capitalize the first word of each sentence and the words listed.

1. Iowa
2. New York; Mississippi River
3. Illinois; Missouri
4. New York City
5. Thanksgiving Day
6. Mount Everest
7. Friday; Thursday
8. January; Paris; France
9. (just first word *In*)
10. April; May; May
11. Santa; Christmas Eve
12. Wisconsin; Saturday
13. Texas; Rio Grande River
14. Tombstone, Arizona; Friday; Friday
15. Devonshire, England
16. Spain; Germany
17. New Mexico

Riddle Answers

1. Neither, they use a spoon.
2. Because he is still alive
3. Glass
4. Times Square
5. Be thankful you're not a turkey.
6. Mount Everest was still the tallest; it just hadn't been discovered yet.
7. In the dictionary
8. They were finished eating.
9. In February, because it's the shortest month.
10. Pilgrims
11 Comet stayed home to clean the sink.
12. They go to the moo-vies.
13. Wet
14. His horse was named Friday.
15. Kittens
16. Neither, they both burn shorter.
17. The horses were too heavy to carry.

Do You Prefer NBA or MLB Games? (p. 15)

1. ASAP - as soon as possible
2. CIA - Central Intelligence Agency
3. COD - cash on delivery
4. GI - government issue
5. IRS - Internal Revenue Service
6. NBC - National Broadcasting Company
7. NFL - National Football League
8. PM - post meridian
9. PS - postscript
10. RN - registered nurse
11. RV - recreational vehicle
12. SCUBA - self-contained underwater breathing apparatus
13. UFO - unidentified flying object
14. VIP - very important person
15. BLT - bacon, lettuce, and tomato
16. FBI - Federal Bureau of Investigation
17. NASA - National Aeronautics and Space Administration

A Little More of This and That (p. 16)

Answers will vary.

Odds and Ends (p. 17)

dear sid,

did you see the baseball history special on tv last night? my favorite story was the one about "shoeless" joe jackson. he began his baseball career as a pitcher, but became an outfielder because his fastball was so forceful it once broke a catcher's arm, and nobody would agree to catch for him.

you knew I was named for stan "the man" musial, the famous rightfielder and first baseman for the st. louis cardinals, didn't you? my middle name, louis, came from the "iron horse," lou gehrig.

my dad played minor league ball for a while and has always been a great baseball fan. he couldn't decide whether to name me ty, after the "georgia peach," ty cobb, or joe, after "joltin'" joe dimaggio. mom refused to consider the name george for george herman ruth because she thought a nickname like "babe" wouldn't be all that great when I grew up.

maybe this summer we can head up to the windy city and watch the cubbies play at wrigley field.

your cousin,
stan

Proofread the Trivia (p. 18)
1. People; Naples, Italy; Neopolitans
2. Some; Embarrass, MN; Square Butt, MT; Echo, TX
3. Did; Walt Disney; Donald Fauntleroy Duck
4. Some; TV; "Batman"; King Tut; Joker; Archer; Black Widow; Mad Hatter; Clock King
5. Adam West; Batman; Burt Ward; Robin; Boy Wonder
6. Andy Griffith; Sheriff Andy Taylor; Emmy; TV; "The Andy Griffith Show"; "Matlock"
7. Don Knotts; Deputy Barney Fife; Emmys
8. Before; Lassie; TV; *Lassie Come Home*; Eric Mowbray Knight
9. Caryn Johnson; Helena Rubenstein Children's Theatre; New York City
10. You; Caryn Johnson; Whoopi Goldberg

Capitalize It Word Search (p. 19)

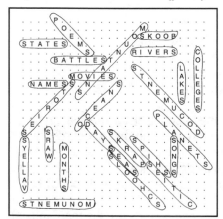

At the End (p. 20)
1. Add question mark.
2. Add exclamation point.
3. Add period.
4. Add question mark.
5. Capitalize *Greek;* add period.
6. Add period.
7. Capitalize *Fill;* add period.
8. Add exclamation point after *Look* and after *already*.
9. Add question mark.
10. Add period.
11. Add exclamation point.
12. Capitalize *Giraffes;* add period.

Commas Separate (p. 21)
1. Thomas Jefferson, born on April 13, 1743, in Shadwell, Virginia, became the third president in March 1801.
2. Jefferson died on July 4, 1826, and was buried at his home near Charlottesville, Virginia.

3. Born in Hyde Park, New Jersey, in January 1882, Franklin D. Roosevelt died on April 12, 1945, shortly after he began his fourth term as president.
4. Three different men served as vice president with Franklin Roosevelt: John N. Garner, Henry A. Wallace, and Harry S Truman.
5. While president, Richard M. Nixon traveled to Moscow, Russia, and Beijing, China.
6. Theodore Roosevelt had six children: Alice, Theodore, Kermit, Ethel, Archibald, and Quentin.

Dendrophobia: A Fear of Trees (p. 22)
1. <u>Barry,</u>
2. <u>Barry,</u>
3. phobias, <u>Barry</u>
4. <u>Santa Claus,</u>
5. shy, <u>Santa,</u>
6. Boston, <u>the city sometimes called Bean Town,</u>
7. Calvin Coolidge, <u>known as Silent Cal,</u>
8. Harriet Tubman, <u>nicknamed the "Moses of her people,"</u>
9. Benjamin Franklin, <u>the man who invented bifocals,</u>
10. Acrophobia, <u>the fear of heights,</u> alektorophobia, <u>the fear of chickens,</u>

Two Into One (p. 23)
Answers may vary. Possible answers given.
1. Abby raked the leaves into piles, and Andy put the leaves into bags.
2. Beth wanted to spend the day at the mall, but she also wanted to spend the day at the beach.
3. Carlos fixed my bicycle, but he could not fix my car.
4. Diane ate three helpings of spaghetti for supper, but she was too full for dessert.
5. Ethan ran a good race, but Ellen finished in first place.
6. Chuck washed the windows of his '57 Chevy, and he checked the oil, but he forgot to fill it with gas.

A Few More Ways to Use Commas (p. 24)
1. cooked,   2. barbecued,
3. ate,   4. bakes,
5. No,   6. vacuum,
7. Santa,   8. truly,
9. left,   10. stopped,

What Did They Say? (p. 25)
1. After serving one term as president, Calvin Coolidge stated, "I do not choose to run for President in 1928."
2. When asked why, Coolidge replied, "Because there's no chance for advancement."

3. "There, I guess King George will be able to read that," stated John Hancock after he signed his name in large letters on the Declaration of Independence.
4. "People who are wrapped up in themselves make small packages," wrote Benjamin Franklin.
5. "Now that I realize what they've had to put up with," wrote Betty Ford about being the first lady, "I have a new respect and admiration for every one of them."

Yogi-isms (p. 26)
1. "A nickel ain't worth a dime anymore," he complained.
2. "It's never happened in World Series history, and it hasn't happened since," Yogi told fans.
3. "It's déjà vu all over again!" he exclaimed.
4. Yogi advised, "When you come to a fork in the road, take it."
5. He also said, "We're lost, but we're making good time."
6. "If I didn't wake up, I'd still be sleeping," he said.
7. Some of Yogi's advice was confusing, like the time he said, "Always go to other people's funerals; otherwise, they won't go to yours."
8. "Little League baseball is a good thing 'cause it keeps the parents off the streets, and it keeps the kids out of the house!" he told a reporter.
9. "The future ain't what it used to be," Yogi said, and I think he was right.

A Dark and Stormy Night (p. 27)
Group 1
A. Delete comma after *Jake*.
B. Correct
C. Replace period with question mark at end of sentence.
D. Add comma after *glasses*.
Group 2
A. Correct
B. Add quotation marks around "Let me out,"
C. Add comma after *flared*.
D. Replace question mark with period at end of sentence.
Group 3
A. Add comma after *thunder*.
B. Add comma after *bed*.
C. Add comma after *bed, dresser, posters, stinky*.
D. Correct

Shouldn't, Wouldn't, Couldn't (p. 28)
2. they're 3. she's
4. we've, they've
5. you'd, she'd, they'd
6. I'll, you'll, we'll, she'll, he'll, they'll
7. didn't 8. shouldn't
9. hadn't 10. won't
11. would + not 12. could + not
13. have + not 14. shall + not

Contraction Action (p. 29)
1. D 2. C 3. C
4. B 5. D 6. B
7. A 8. B 9. A
10. C

What's Your Favorite Phobia? (p. 30)
1. aren't 2. I've 3. He's
4. won't 5. would've 6. she'll
7. doesn't 8. Don't 9. You'd
10. they're 11. shouldn't 12. What's; It's

Fine as Frog's Fur (p. 31)
1. the man's monkeys
2. Oscar's orange octopus
3. Dr. Seuss's stories
4. a child's grandparents
5. Agnes's aches
6. a fly's wings
7. a zebra's stripes
8. Pat's pajamas
9. a mouse's houses
10. a goose's eggs

Are There Mice in Their Houses? (p. 32)
1. the geese's eggs
2. the woman's clubs
3. the women's club
4. the birds' nests
5. the grandparents' grandchildren
6. the fly's eyes
7. the flies' eyes
8. the mice's houses

They Lost Their Snake (p. 33)
1. hers 2. her 3. mine
4. my 5. yours 6. your
7. its 8. his 9. their
10. theirs

It's Time to Call the Vet (p. 34)

1.	It's; its	2.	You're; your
3.	They're; their	4.	theirs; there's
5.	It's	6.	your
7.	There's	8.	its
9.	you're	10.	their
11.	theirs	12.	there's

Gus's Goose (p. 35)
Nouns will vary.

1.	child's	2.	woman's
3.	Rosie's	4.	group's
5.	squirrel's	6.	crowds'
7.	men's	8.	leaves'
9.	glasses'	10.	aardvarks'
11.	person's	12.	singer's
13.	frog's	14.	kitty's
15.	Cathy's	16.	foxes'
17.	monkeys'	18.	kitties'
19.	daisies'	20.	wolves'

Introducing: The Colon (p. 36)

1.	reason:	2.	Hawaii:
3.	saw:	4.	enjoyed:
5.	together:	6.	no colon needed
7.	no colon needed	8.	state:
9.	states:	10.	time:

Five More Ways to Use a Colon (p. 37)

1. 3:45
2. Proverbs 24:26
3. *Seabiscuit: An American Legend*
4. Dear Mr. President:
5. (*Twelfth Night* II:5)
6. Answers will vary.

Connector and Super Comma (p. 38)

1.	sheep,	2.	alone;
3.	lamb;	4.	clock, and
5.	laughed;	6.	meadow,
7.	nimble;	8.	hill,
9.	cockleshells,	10.	shoe,

Don't Wait to Punctuate (p. 39)

1. I'll pick you up at 7:30—no, make it 7:10—and we'll go rock climbing.
2. The pilot flew to Rome, Italy; Frankfurt, Germany; Paris, France; and London, England, last week.
3. Let's follow the west trail—or would you rather not?
4. All the people from the village—men, women, children—joined the animals fleeing the out-of-control fire.
5. Lincoln was a tall man who wore a top hat—a most unusual sight to be sure.
6. I'd like a chocolate shake—better make that a diet soda—I'm trying to lose weight.
7. Dear Library Director:
8. Would you please order more historical fiction like *The Black Flower: A Novel of the Civil War* for our library?

How Does Your Garden Grow? (p. 40)
Answers will vary.

Let's Review (p. 41)

1.	K	2.	M	3.	L
4.	B	5.	F	6.	A
7.	D	8.	C	9.	E
10.	N	11.	H	12.	J
13.	I	14.	P	15.	O
16.	G				